BOOMERABILIA

BOOMERABILIA

I REMEMBER...

JUDY GORDON MORROW

BROADMAN
&HOLMAN
PUBLISHERS

Nashville, Tennessee

© 1998
by Judy Gordon Morrow
All rights reserved
Printed in the United States of America

0-8054-1275-1

Published by Broadman & Holman Publishers, Nashville, Tennessee
Acquisitions and Development Editor: Vicki Crumpton
Page Design: Anderson Thomas Design
Typesetting: Desktop Miracles

Dewey Decimal Classification: 305.24
Subject Heading: BABY BOOM GENERATION
Library of Congress Card Catalog Number: 98-6675

Library of Congress Cataloging-in-Publication Data

Morrow, Judy Gordon.
    Boomerabilia: I remember / Judy Gordon Morrow
      p. cm.
    ISBN 0-8054-1275-1
    1. Baby boom generation—United States—Miscellanea. 2. Nineteen fifties—Miscellanea. 3. Nineteen sixties—Miscellanea. I. Title.
HN78.M67   1998
305.24'0973'09045—dc21

98-6675
CIP

1 2 3 4 5 02 01 00 99 98

 **DEDICATION**

WITH LOVE TO MY
BABY BOOMER SISTERS,
NANCY GORDON AND
BECKY GORDON COBB—
THANKS FOR THE
FOND MEMORIES.

AND IN LOVING MEMORY
OF OUR BROTHER,
JIM GORDON
1949-1993

ACKNOWLEDGMENTS

THANK YOU TO THE FOLLOWING BABY BOOMERS FOR THEIR REMINISCES:

ESTELLE BEER
MELODY CARLSON
CAROL DAVIS
NANCY GORDON
JANET KOBOBEL GRANT
SUSAN JACKSON
LEE WARDLAW JAFFURS
REBECCA PRICE JANNEY
JOHN KIMMEL
PAULINE KIMMEL
LINDA MARTIN

GAIL MCCORMICK
CRAIG MCHENRY
JANET HOLM MCHENRY
PATRICK MORROW
CHRISTINE PETERS
ROBERT TURCOTTE
JOAN TURNER
SHERYL VERNOR
WILLIAM VERNOR
JEANNE WILLIAMS
PATRICIA WORK

I remember wearing my Davy Crockett coonskin hat while I watched his show on TV.

I remember bouffant hairdos that were never mussed by the wind.

I remember five-and-dime
stores with hardwood floors
and ceiling fans.

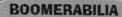

I remember the comedian, Bill Dana,
who came on The Ed Sullivan Show
and said, "My name Jose Jimenez."

I remember my parents talking
in hushed tones about my
uncle's concrete, underground
"barn." Years later I learned
it was a bomb shelter.

I remember our high school
principal calling boys into his
office and measuring to make
sure their hair was high
enough above their collars.

I remember the funny radio
commercials for Gorilla Milk.

I remember seeing the
peace sign everywhere.

I remember Burma Shave signs
along the side of the road.

I remember test patterns on
TV if we got up before Saturday
morning cartoons started.

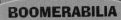
I remember as a sixth grader
feeling proud to be on our
elementary school's Safety Patrol.
I wore a yellow helmet and belt
and extended my yellow flag to
let children cross the street.

I remember olive green, shag carpet and plastic carpet rakes.

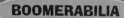

I remember watching The Ed Sullivan Show the first time the Beatles sang on TV. Wow!

I remember when the answer was "Blowin' in the Wind."

I remember the sad stories told by women as they vied to become Queen for a Day.

I remember telephone
party lines and listening for
the right number of rings.

I remember frosted white
lipstick, thick black eyeliner,
and peroxided hair that turned
green after swimming.

I remember drinking
a Goldwater soda.

I remember my grandmother
mending our socks, using her
darning egg and thimble.

I remember my brown Beatle boots with a zipper on the side.

I remember my dad lining up our shoes on newspapers on Saturday night so he could polish them for church the next day.

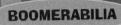
I remember pastel pop-beads.

I remember the big boom when
I hit a whole roll of caps for my
cap gun with a rock or hammer.

I remember wax lips on Halloween.

I remember stores with penny candy. My favorites were chewy nickels and mint licorice.

I remember President Kennedy's
assassination and how my brother
got his toy soldiers so we could
make a funeral procession as we
watched the real one on TV.

I remember that my second grade teacher, who had always been very stern, broke down and cried when John F. Kennedy was shot.

I remember three-year-old "John John" Kennedy saluting his father's casket.

I remember Robert Kennedy's
assassination in June 1968.

I remember getting my hair
caught in the car door
during a Chinese fire drill.

I remember the sound
baseball cards made in
the spokes of my bike.

I remember slipping all over the
gymnasium floor during a sock hop.

I remember listening to the
Apollo 10 astronauts read
the Creation story from Genesis
on Christmas Eve, 1968, as they
orbited the moon and sent
pictures back to earth.

I remember hamburger stands
that looked like hamburgers.

I remember having two pairs
of shoes, one for school and
one for church.

I remember split windshields
and big chrome fenders.

I remember my brother, sister,
and I pulling our red wagon
around the neighborhood
for a mobile lemonade stand.

I remember I quit biting
my fingernails because my
grandmother promised me a penny
for each finger that grew out a nail.

I remember St. Joseph's aspirin for children and their commercial with the little boy asking, "Can Judy come out to play?"

I remember feeling really chic in my new capri pants.

I remember Viewmasters
with slides of the seven wonders
of the ancient world.

I remember peanut butter and
jelly tailgate picnics on the side
of the road on the way to
Grandma and Grandpa's house.

I remember folding pirate hats from newspapers.

I remember when my parents bought a red Plymouth Valiant, the first push-button transmission car.

I remember "Good night,
David. Good night, Chet."

I remember my little
glow-in-the-dark plastic cross
from Vacation Bible School
and how I took it to bed with me.

I remember listening to the Beach Boys on my brother's portable record player in the dead of a New Jersey winter.

I remember my father's tears when I left for the service in 1968.

I remember hearing every morning on the radio how many soldiers were killed that day in Vietnam. Then the station would play "The Ballad of the Green Berets."

I remember sending Christmas cards and comics to two soldiers in Vietnam.

I remember wearing a
silver **MIA** bracelet.

I remember trying to be creative
when I wrote to my brother in
Vietnam. I wrote on toilet paper,
paper towels, and popsicle sticks.
He was jealous of the guy beside
him who got romantic letters.

I remember learning that
a high school friend had
been killed in Vietnam.

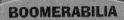

I remember college administration
buildings being bombed in
protest of the Vietnam War.

I remember sending a friend,
who was serving in Vietnam, a
huge box of Bazooka bubble
gum so he could give pieces to
the kids on the streets. He said
they loved it and that it was a hoot
to see them try to blow bubbles.

I remember all the letters
I got in Vietnam addressed
"To any serviceman."

I remember the ballad, "Where
Have All the Flowers Gone?"

I remember my first Christmas in Vietnam, the first Christmas away from my family. I received my care package from home on Christmas Eve. It contained an artificial tree, ornaments, and a Frosty the Snowman filled with candy.

I remember sliding back and forth on the seats of our '57 station wagon and singing the echo part of "By the Light of the Silvery Moon" with our parents.

I remember flannelgraph Bible stories in Sunday school.

I remember standing behind
our long, wooden stereo cabinet
and lip syncing the words to
an entire Andy Williams album.

I remember my first Barbie doll.

I remember yearning for
a blue 427 Cobra.

I remember making papier-mache
animals from flour and water.

I remember playing Pegity, Flinch, and Anagrams with my grandma.

I remember Saturday nights when our family sat in front of the television eating TV dinners that came in foil trays.

I remember my brother's
Triumph convertible and the
night he took my entire slumber
party out for a spin around
the block, in it and on it!

I remember being scratched
to death by the pink mohair
sweater my mom knit me.

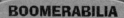

I remember that Sambo's
Coffee Shop was my
favorite pancake place.

I remember my mom painting two
large paint-by-number pictures of
Jesus as our Shepherd and hanging
them in our living room.

I remember Cokes for 10¢
and hamburgers for 19¢!

I remember that we were
playing outside one Tuesday
night, when just before 7:00 a
bat flew by and we remembered
it was time to watch Batman.

I remember my go-go boots and how they smelled after a rainy day.

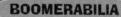

I remember when no stores were open on Sunday because it was a day set aside for church and rest.

I remember sawing my skateboard
in half and attaching the wheels
to our wooden ironing board
so that three or four kids
could ride at the same time.

I remember getting off the bus
at school and rolling up my skirt
at the waist so I could be in style.

I remember bright orange-red
Merthiolate that burned like
crazy when my dad put it on my
scrapes and scratches.

I remember getting a Twiggy
haircut when I was twelve,
and some boys asking me
if I was a girl or a boy!

I remember wearing my first pair of fishnet hosiery. By the end of the day they had a hole so big that a marlin could have swum through!

I remember that every time I took off my GI Joe's boot, his foot would come off, too.

I remember that in junior high all the boys on campus wore blue jeans and white T-shirts.

I remember the Maypole Dance on May 1 with all the different colored streamers and the girls wearing pretty dresses.

I remember saving **S&H Green Stamps** and **Blue Chip Stamps** that came with our grocery receipts. We kids licked them and put them into the savings books, which could be spent at the redemption store. We got our **TV trays** there.

I remember macrame lampshades, purses, chairs, and plant hangers.

I remember when the rage was to melt and shape LPs into bowls with scalloped edges, and then fill them with wax fruit. My mom made our bowl from a red LP.

I remember stretch pants that didn't stay up when you bent over.

I remember Captain Kangaroo, Bunny Rabbit, and especially Mr. Green Jeans.

I remember making stacks
of cinnamon toast after school
and washing it all down with
Nestle Quik chocolate milk while
watching The Bowery Boys and
The Three Stooges on TV.

I remember when boys' swim
trunks were just cut-off blue jeans.

I remember the sock monkey
my grandma made me with
work socks that you could only
buy at Montgomery Ward.

I remember the pungent smells
made by the woodburning set my
brother got one Christmas.

I remember when it was a
big deal that a doll could drink,
wet and blink her eyes.

I remember "boy watcher"
sunglasses and John Lennon hats.

I remember my first love at the tender age of ten—Paul McCartney. I traded any Beatle card, or anything else I owned, for a Paul McCartney Beatle card.

I remember Mike Nelson in Sea Hunt.

I remember arguing with my girlfriend about who was cooler— Elvis Presley or Paul McCartney. Paul definitely was!

I remember when teasing was something done to girls' hair.

I remember when the name
"Edsel" made everyone snicker.

I remember the sound
of coffee percolating.

I remember Memorial Day parades.

I remember learning the
names of famous writers
and their books from playing
Authors, the card game.

I remember the smell of white paste and the plastic applicator that was attached inside the lid.

I remember the unrest and shootings at Kent State.

I remember singing every verse of "Found a Peanut" on long car trips.

I remember replaying the 45 record of "The Ballad of Bonnie and Clyde" until my cousin threatened to break it.

I remember Gunsmoke with Matt, Doc, Kitty, and Chester.

I remember the little boy's voice on the hot cereal commercial saying, "I want my Maypo."

I remember debating with my friend which were better, cherry Cokes or lemon Cokes.

I remember the way Linus said, "And they were sore afraid" of the angels in A Charlie Brown Christmas.

I remember playing Mouse Trap,
Chutes and Ladders, and Old Maid.

I remember tight girdles
and bumpy garters.

I remember buying Bazooka
bubble gum for 1¢.

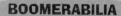

I remember practicing fire
drills at school and also for
air raids when we would
"duck and cover" under our
desks while the loud siren wailed.

I remember the "evil" Russian
ruler, Nikita Kruschev.

I remember when it was considered
more proper to say a woman
was "expecting" or "pg" than
to use the word "pregnant."

I remember in grade school through high school when boys asked girls to "go steady" with them.

I remember sandals called retreads that were made out of tires.

I remember wrapping my steady's class ring with mohair yarn so it would fit my finger. I bought yarn of many colors to match my outfits.

I remember when my mom gave me a book with a plain brown paper cover that explained the "facts of life."

I remember when the public school Christmas programs were filled with traditional, sacred carols.

I remember gasoline
for 19¢ a gallon.

I remember sprinkling and rolling up
our cotton clothes, then leaving
them in a plastic bag until we could
iron them. Sometimes we waited
too long, and they got moldy!

I remember reading every
Nancy Drew book.

I remember loving the rare
opportunities to get into our
old trunk kept out in the garage
and looking at the stored
memories such as my father's
World War II army uniform.

I remember kneeling on the floor at school to see if my dress was long enough.

I remember photo albums with the little black paper corners to hold the photos in place, and how the corners often came unglued and fell off.

I remember wearing corduroy pants under my dresses for warmth and so I could play on the swings and bars during recess.

I remember the huge, warm cinnamon rolls served in our school cafeteria.

I remember wearing an ugly, brown hairnet when I worked in the school cafeteria. The free lunches really helped our family. And I loved Fridays when we got free ice cream, too.

I remember my first transistor radio; it even had an earphone.

I remember the British Invasion
of singers, especially Chad and
Jeremy, Herman's Hermits, and
Gerry and the Pacemakers.

I remember that we bought the new
and more expensive color film for
photographing special events.

I remember Youth for Christ
rallies on Saturday nights.

I remember looking for VW Beetles
on trips, calling out "Slug Bug"
and socking the person nearest to
me on the shoulder. The person
with the most sightings won.

I remember Paladin in
Have Gun Will Travel and the
white knight on his holster.

I remember, "Look, Mom,
no cavities!"

I remember a Crest commercial that I can still quote to this day: "Crest has been shown to be an effective decay preventative dentifrice that can be of significant value when used in a conscientiously applied program of oral hygiene and regular professional care."

I remember the summer my
mom made me pastel pedal
pushers with floral tops to match.

I remember baby-sitting six
kids for 50¢ an hour.

I remember silver taps
on the guys' black shoes.

I remember Peter, Paul,
and Mary; The Kingston Trio;
and the New Christy Minstrels.

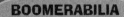

I remember tent dresses and how they billowed when the wind caught them just right.

I remember ballroom dancing in junior high and how there were three girls for every guy.

I remember knowing the
next program was going to
be in color when the animated
peacock fanned its wings on TV.

I remember watching
The Twilight Zone with my mom
on Friday nights and drinking hot
cocoa out of a fancy china cup.

I remember operetta productions
in junior high and high school.
In seventh grade I was a
Munchkin in The Wizard of Oz.

I remember setting my balsa plane
on fire and flying it out my window.

I remember "Smile,
you're on Candid Camera!"

I remember playing "paper tag"
on our bikes. We'd throw
newspapers at each other's bikes,
and then that person was "it."

I remember my dad not
allowing me to wear jeans
because they were "men's pants."

I remember Bonanza, Rawhide,
and Wagon Train.

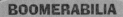
I remember when my
sixth-grade teacher read
A Wrinkle in Time to our class.

I remember burning paper trash in
our incinerator can in the backyard.

I remember week-long revival services at our church every spring and fall.

I remember handsome
Dr. Kildare and stern **Ben Casey.**

I remember Chinese jump rope.

I remember heating a nail to make "bullet holes" in my model airplane.

I remember Dick Van Dyke always
tripping over the ottoman and his
pretty TV wife, Mary Tyler Moore.

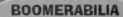

I remember graham crackers
and milk before naptime
in kindergarten.

I remember the clicking sound
of the classroom film projector,
and how it would break down
at least once during the film.

I remember fierce playground
games of four square.

I remember Planet of the Apes.

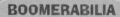

I remember wishing I could be one
of the kids on Romper Room. I still
have my plastic Do Bee hat.

I remember when you had to
go to a doctor to get your ears
pierced, unless you were brave
and tried the ice and ice pick
method with a friend.

I remember Dippity Doo hair gel
and Brylcreem, of which
"a little dab will do ya."

I remember having a sticky
neck from candy necklaces.

I remember wearing a dandelion
halo in my hair and praying for
peace at a college sit-in.

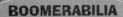
I remember when Alaska
and Hawaii were not states.

I remember when Elvis
Presley enlisted in the Army.

I remember when Jim Ryun
was the first man to run the mile
in under four minutes in 1966.

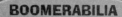

I remember when the Man in
Black, Johnny Cash, sang
"A Boy Named Sue."

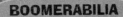

I remember doing well
on everything except pull-ups
in President Kennedy's
Physical Fitness Test.

I remember wearing
sweatshirts inside out.

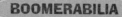

I remember lining up at
school in two lines—boys in one
line, girls in the other—shortest
in the front to tallest at back.

I remember the Schwinn Monarch
bikes with the front spring forks.

I remember clothes made
from bleeding Madras fabric.

I remember eating dinner at
exactly 5:30 every night with all
family members present.

I remember when we
sewed most of our clothes.

I remember when the postal
service started using **ZIP** codes.

I remember we had the
first color TV in the neighborhood.

I remember buying 45s for
99¢ at Woolworth's.

I remember attending a Billy Graham Crusade in Fresno. I bought a snow cone and was eating away, when to my horror, the top flew off and went down the back of the woman sitting in front of me.

I remember my mom pulling my
hair back so tight for a ponytail
that my eyes looked slanted.

I remember playing the games
Red Light, Green Light,
Mother, May I? and
Drop the Handkerchief.

I remember sitting in the middle of the back seat of the car and having to perch my feet on the hump.

I remember what a treat it was to buy a little white bag of chocolate stars when we shopped at Sears.

I remember trying to make
my 25¢ allowance last all week.

I remember Route 66, The Fugitive,
and 77 Sunset Strip.

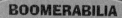
I remember stylish baby
blue Princess telephones.

I remember my collection of
stretch hairbands; I had a
matching one for every outfit.

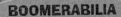
I remember sending away
for Mr. Peanut stuff with
empty 5¢ bags.

I remember Betsy McCall
paper dolls.

I remember the Helms Bakery
truck whistle and the
messy jelly doughnuts.

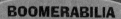

I remember watching my
Water Wiggle get stuck on
our TV antenna the
very first time I tried it.

I remember not being able to sleep after watching The Birds.

I remember praying for the Apollo 13 astronauts and writing a poem in the midst of that tense situation. I still have the poem.

I remember fishing for bullheads
in the crick (not the creek).

I remember using aluminum
reflectors during our high
school lunch time to get a
faster tan on our faces.

I remember mixing baby oil and iodine to enhance our tans.

I remember that sneakers were only for gym class and the one-piece outfits we wore with bloomer shorts.

I remember when letters
cost 5¢ to mail.

I remember wringer
washing machines.

I remember getting prizes from the shoe store. I loved the prize eggs from Mother Goose shoes.

I remember my daddy preaching at my baccalaureate. He did a great job, and I was so proud.

I remember singing
"Happy Trails to You" with
Roy Rogers and Dale Evans.

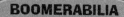

I remember storing gallon jugs of
water and extra food in a large
inner closet in case Russia bombed
nearby Spokane, Washington.

I remember that all the cheerleaders wore black and white saddle shoes.

I remember my first baseball glove was a J. C. Higgins, when what I really wanted was a Spalding or a Wilson.

I remember when telephone
numbers were only five digits long.

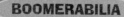

I remember when you made
popcorn in a pan on the stove.

I remember standing in line at school for my booster shots.

I remember chains made of chewing gum wrappers.

I remember my brother trying to recreate the Swiss Family Robinson tree house.

I remember learning how to wash windows, sew an apron, and iron clothes in Home Ec. class.

I remember when she wore an
"Itsy Bitsy Teeny Weeny
Yellow Polka Dot Bikini."

I remember my grandma's
homemade doughnuts.

I remember when dishwashers came out and only the newest and most expensive homes had them.

I remember there was a time in high school when we wore pegged pants skin tight. We could barely walk or sit down, but our pants had to be this way.

I remember staying up late to dance to the theme from Mission Impossible.

I remember X-ray machines at shoe stores to see if shoes fit correctly.

I remember gas station giveaways.

I remember not being able
to decide which one I wanted
to pretend to be, Ginger or
Mary Ann or Betty or Veronica.

I remember pixie haircuts
and Tonette perms.

I remember making music
by humming on a comb
covered with wax paper.

I remember always wearing
a coat and tie to church.

I remember that the best thing
to use playing potsy (hopscotch)
was a metal, links key chain
because it wouldn't bounce
or slide out of the box.

I remember when Wilt Chamberlain scored 100 points in a game in 1962.

I remember crying during Lassie each week and wanting a dog just like her.

I remember bruises from the Slip and Slide, not to mention our destroyed lawn.

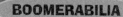

I remember family camping before there were campgrounds.

I remember when sports programs did not have instant replay.

I remember watching Peggy Fleming as a teenage ice skater and just loving her.

Dear Reader, I realize one little book can't possibly hold all the fond remembrances of baby boomers. If you were born in the years of 1946-1965 and would like to contribute your own "boomerabilia" for a possible future edition, I'd welcome your "I remember" memories. All submissions become the property of the author and all rights thereto, including copyrights. Please be sure to include your name for the acknowledgments page. Thank you!

Judy Gordon Morrow
P. O. Box 3057
Quincy, CA 95971
jmorrow@inreach.com